Michael Barnfather's
DERBYSHIRE

Michael Barnfather's
DERBYSHIRE

Peter Slade

HALSGROVE
IN ASSOCIATION WITH
GRANBY GALLERY

First published in 2002 by Halsgrove
Images © 2002 Michael Barnfather
Text © 2002 Peter Slade

British Library Cataloguing-in-Publication Data
A CIP record for this title is available from the British Library

ISBN 1 84114 187 9

HALSGROVE
Halsgrove House
Lower Moor Way
Tiverton, Devon EX16 6SS
T: 01884 243242
F: 01884 243325
www.halsgrove.com

Printed in Hong Kong
by Regal Printing Ltd

Contents

Foreword   7

Introduction   9

Life and Times   11

Publications   17

A Gallery-Owner Recalls   27

Approach to Painting   29

The Paintings   35

I would like to express my thanks to all those collectors who allowed me access to their paintings; to Jim Fardon and Michael Mosley for their highly personal contributions; and, of course, to Michael Barnfather himself for his time and perseverence.

Foreword

I was all of forty years old when I accompanied Michael on a sketching trip and he taught me to look more closely at our English landscape. Like most people I could always admire a beautiful view of the countryside, but until this point I had not really noticed just how changed the same scene could appear at different times of the day, or in another season. We were looking for suitable subjects for a regional exhibition and we had stopped early in the morning to look at a village that seemed just right for one of his canvasses. He studied it for a short while but said that we should come back in the afternoon, by which time, the sun, coming from another direction, had transformed a good picture into a captivating one. This is his gift. Later the same day, in order to gain a better vantage point for a scene he had in mind, he suddenly jumped down into the dry bed of a stream. I just could not possibly imagine it as a finished work but it turned out to be the most sought-after canvas in the show!

Since then, over thirty years, I have enjoyed Michael's friendship and the opportunity of seeing most of his pictures, and in all of them he demonstrates his skill in drawing and perspective, his observation of small detail, and his canny choice of subject matter. Yet, I believe that what mostly attracts his large following is not just his technical ability but also something else, something which stands out in all his paintings. This is his inherent love of the landscape. The word inherent is perhaps the right one, as it was his grandfather, a keen walker, who would take the budding artist on long treks through his native county of Derbyshire, initially stirring his interest. Maybe it is why he is so well known for his speciality – his wide panoramic all-encompassing vistas – first seen through the wondering eyes of a young boy.

He passes on his enthusiasm by painting the countryside in all its moods; and in every image there is usually some delightful detail. A winter scene may divulge a fox slipping almost unnoticed along a hedge; another picture might show an old Ferguson tractor spending its retirement in a farmer's barn. Very occasionally one may see what can be described as 'a little amatory interest'. However, in each of them you will find another bit of detail, a broken branch, which Michael likes to paint in by way of an additional signature.

It would be wrong to assume that every picture that came from an artist's easel was his finest work, but very few of Michael Barnfather's paintings come into a category of less than nine out of ten, and his Derbyshire landscapes, depicting some of the most beautiful views in England, do seem to be among the very best that he paints.

Jim Fardon
Alexander Gallery

Introduction

As Jim Fardon has stated in his foreword, the paths of Michael Barnfather and Alexander Gallery have been intertwined for over thirty years. In this time virtually every picture that Michael has painted has passed through our hands on its way to some eager collector; each a separate record of the topography of England and the effect on that landscape of the ever-changing seasons.

Although Michael's work is instantly recognisable, like most artists he remains a largely anonymous figure who to all intents and purposes appears as if by magic only at exhibition Private Views! This, of course, is not strictly true but the nature of an artist is mainly a solitary one; sketching and exploring may be undertaken in company but applying paint to canvas is strictly a solo pursuit.

Thus whilst a collector is able to enjoy his or her painting or paintings over a period of time, and get to know them very much in the way the artist gets to know his subject, the relationship between artist and patron is nearly always somewhat removed. The purpose of this book therefore is to bridge this gap between the two by revealing a little about Michael Barnfather the man, as well as celebrating his fruitful relationship with his home county of Derbyshire.

Peter Slade
Alexander Gallery
July 2002

Life and Times

'I paint because I enjoy it and when I look back there never seems to have been a time when I wasn't painting.'

After almost forty years as a professional artist Michael Barnfather is firmly established as one of the country's leading landscape painters. A love of the rural scene forged at an early age has inspired this dedicated man to devote most of his adult life to recording the ever-changing moods and shapes of the British countryside.

Michael was born in Ilkeston, nine miles north of Derby, to Leslie and Doris Barnfather in 1934, into a family with a strong artistic vein already running through it. Leslie was an enthusiastic amateur and on his mother's side Michael's great-grandfather was an accomplished stonemason whose work can still be seen adorning municipal buildings in Nottingham. Michael's maternal grandfather, Grandpa Hunter, was also a proficient watercolourist ,who decorated his own house with skilled copies of old masters. The family tradition did not stop with Michael; his younger brother Geoffrey ultimately becoming a leading light at Cumbria College of Art & Design where he was responsible for the introduction of the Fine Art Degree course. Although the course covered all aspects of fine art it was sculpture that Geoffrey himself specialised in.

However, the most significant family influence on Michael came from his paternal grandfather, David Barnfather. He was a well-known amateur painter from Chesterfield who regularly exhibited his land-scape paintings in the town. David's influence on his young grandson was twofold; not only did he introduce him to the environment of a regular painter but he also introduced him to the idea of observing the countryside from a painter's point of view. Michael was a regular weekend visitor to his grand-father's house in Holymoorside and, when the weather permitted, they spent much of their time together walking in the surrounding countryside.

These walks would usually take them through or past small villages and farms, often following the course of a river or stream. These were the subjects that his grandfather painted and this was the point at which Michael's real interest in painting the countryside really began.

To improve on his early efforts, and to learn more about the basics of composition and technique, Michael began attending an art club in Belper attended by Harry Topliss, a well-known watercolourist from

Matlock. He helped Michael with composition and under his influence and guidance Michael began painting landscapes in watercolours. Harry Topliss also introduced him to working and sketching in the field.

Cartoon self-portrait – Rolls Royce Drawing Office

In 1950 Michael began attending Derby College of Art and in 1952 joined Rolls Royce in Derby as an apprentice technical illustrator, specialising in air-brush work, on cutaway drawings of aero engines for maintenance manuals. At this stage he had no thoughts of becoming an artist although he continued with his watercolours, many of which were signed 'Barny'. In the time-honoured tradition these were purchased by family and friends. However the subject matter had somehow undergone a dramatic change. Exotic Spanish street scenes replaced Derbyshire landscapes. These mainly imaginative subjects were painted in a highly individual format of 21 inches high by 5 inches wide to emphasise the narrowness of the

streets. This technique of unusually proportioned pictures has remained one of Michael's idiosyncratic trademarks to this day.

Not content with selling to friends and family, Michael approached several local galleries to see if they would like to handle his work and was delighted when he was accepted by a gallery in Derby. This was his first foray into selling to a dealer and was very successful for both parties.

National Service in 1955 interrupted his apprenticeship when Michael was called up for the RAF where he served as an aircraftsman first class at Turnhill, near Shrewsbury. Working mainly in the control tower he was responsible for a crude form

Female study

Male study – RAF

of air traffic control, logging aircraft on take-off and landing, passing on air pressure settings and 'losing aircraft most days'. In a variation on Brian Hanrahan's famous Falklands War statement of 'counting them out and counting them back in again,' Michael often had to excuse himself from the control tower on the pretext of a toilet break, run to the hangars and see which aircraft had landed unrecorded. Returning to the control tower he would then mark up the relevant chart to confirm that they had returned safely! Fortunately, he still found time to continue his art studies at Shrewsbury College of Art, concentrating on life studies.

After completing National Service in 1957 he returned to Rolls Royce but left two years later and moved to Bristol where he took a post with a small illustration studio. Working extensively with an airbrush he continued with technical illustration, but also found himself working in packaging, enhancing the designs on the covers of packets of ladies' corsets! A further move soon followed to another studio which gave him a broader remit, touching in and colouring line drawings and photographs of building interiors, including atomic energy power stations and post offices. Although all this was more varied and artistic than the earlier technical work, it was not as satisfying to him as his painting which he continued whenever and wherever possible.

During this time he was returning to Derbyshire most weekends to see his fiancée Ann Bell who lived in Belper. They married in 1963 and purchased a house in Bristol, in Patchway, ironically not far from the Rolls Royce factory at Filton.

It was about this time that he moved away from watercolours and first began experimenting with oil paints. He immediately found them more satisfying than watercolour and particularly enjoyed the effect of applying several layers of paint to create depth and add texture to the picture. It also enabled him to build up pictures and work on a much larger scale than before. By its nature, watercolour is a spontaneous medium and the necessary speed of application was not suited to the large and complex pictures Michael was by now wanting to paint. At the same time he abandoned the street scenes and returned to more traditional landscape subjects.

Although happy in his work at the design studio, he felt more and more assured in his painting and in 1964 he took the decision to turn professional. Not every amateur artist is capable of making the move from part-time hobby to full time career without some anxieties but Michael was confident enough in his own abilities to do so. One person who encouraged him greatly at this time was fellow artist Deborah Jones, now famous for her paintings of teddy bears, street scenes and still life. She and Michael had become friends after meeting at the Clifton Art Club in Bristol and he remembers that she was very positive about his decision to paint full time.

Now without the need to live in Bristol, Michael and Ann decided to leave the city and they moved across the Severn to a cottage in Tidenham near Chepstow. This move necessitated the purchase of a motorcycle to avoid lengthy delays queuing for the ferry, the only quick way to South Wales prior to the opening of the first Severn Bridge in 1967.

Although he had dabbled in abstract work, something he returns to from time to time as a complete change, he had by now found an approach that satisfied him. Working to a long thin format of around 12 inches high by 46 inches wide he painted country panoramas of farm and village scenes. Most of these early works are painted on board because specially made canvasses to such non-standard sizes were at that time difficult to obtain and were prohibitively expensive. Another feature of these early works was the vividly coloured skies of bright yellow, pink and even green. Michael admits now that he has no idea where these colours came from but suggests that he felt that he wanted to give a bit of life to what was a very traditional subject, albeit presented in the unusual panoramic format. On this aspect of his painting he is more certain, 'I wanted to record more than just a farm or a church; I wanted to show the whole village and the way it fitted into the natural landscape.'

Having settled on a style and subject that he was happy with he spent most of his spare time travelling, both to look for subjects, and possible outlets for his paintings. He still regularly visited Derbyshire to see his parents and would take the opportunity to visit galleries to show his work. He established a good relationship with Pratts of Derby, which was the leading gallery in the town, and they became one of his most successful outlets over many years. Several of Mr Pratt's clients built up a collection of more than a dozen of Michael's paintings, leading at one stage to the proposed formation by a number of lady clients of a Michael Barnfather fan club. On recently being reminded of this, Michael dryly commented, 'I don't think I encouraged it.'

Sketch– Alport, Derbyshire

Back in Bristol he began showing with June Macpherson at her gallery in Clifton village and at the Brights of Bristol department store, in a picture gallery concession run by leading London art dealers Frost & Reed who were based in Bristol. Michael was invited to show at Brights by Frost & Reed executive Jim Fardon and when he left F & R in 1969 to open Alexander Gallery, Michael was one of the first artists that Jim invited to join him. This highly successful partnership between artist and gallery continues to this day.

After their two children Aaron and Fleur were born in 1970 and 1971 the family moved to Cribau Mill, an isolated farmhouse situated in a valley between Llanvair Discoed and Shirenewton. Michael had a purpose-built studio erected in the grounds and Ann ran a small B & B from the house. The children were cared for with help from a succession of au pairs, several of which became models for some of Michael's figurative works. One of these, Alex, later became well known in Europe as a leading Paris-based fashion model. The family remained at Cribau Mill until Michael and Ann's divorce in 1993 but Michael still lives and works in South Wales.

In 1984 Michael wrote about his life as a painter in an exhibition catalogue and took the opportunity to point out that the life of an artist is susceptible to the same trials and tribulations as everyone else:

An interesting commission arrived one day from a titled couple in Scotland, whose home was a castle and they invited me to stay while I worked on the picture. They were delightful hosts and on the first night we dined in splendour served by the butler from a plentiful variety of silverware. The next day his lordship accompanied by his beautifully trained gundogs drove his Land Rover, with me following with my car and equipment and packed lunch, to a nearby mountain. This was the point from which the best but rather distant view of the castle could be seen.

I had taken a large canvas that just fitted the back ledge of the car, so I could draw the picture straight out. I spent all day working out the design, which was made doubly difficult by the distance of the castle, and I had to keep lifting binoculars up and down to pick up certain detail. Suffice to say by the time the Land Rover returned in the evening to guide me back, I had had a hard concentrated day, but had done a good day's work and had secured everything safely in the car. Imagine my shock however, when one of the labradors, trained to go into a car and sit obediently on the back ledge jumped in through the open rear door, clawed the canvas out of the way and sat on the back ledge looking very pleased with himself! He totally destroyed the canvas with his claw marks and all that effort was wasted.

My hosts could not have been more apologetic and I must say that after a few drinks and the promise of another good dinner, I had resigned myself to the sad fact of having to do it all over again.

However, whether it was the drink or the tragedy of the picture that was responsible for what followed, I don't know. At dinner that night there was no butler but there was a sumptuous meal, all set out in covered silver dishes on the sideboard and we helped ourselves. As the guest I went first and as I uncovered each dish in turn all these delicious treats were revealed, and the last of these was a tall silver jug full of gravy. Now I'm very partial to this and gave myself a liberal helping, whereupon Lady ___ exclaimed, 'Mr Barnfather, do you normally put chocolate sauce on your meat?'

Other eventful painting trips have resulted in Michael being mistaken for a motorway planner by an irate and armed farmer convinced a road was being planned through his land; and the occasion when he had to fish for lost car keys down a grating using a rod and line with a magnet on the end!

Today, two years short of his seventieth birthday, a milestone that will coincide with forty years as a professional painter, Michael admits to taking life a little easier. Working almost exclusively for his biannual exhibitions with Alexander Gallery and Granby Gallery he is now devoting more time to himself, his partner Meg and to his sporting pursuits of golf, tennis and skiing. He maintains a healthy interest in the work of other artists and is particularly fond of figurative paintings and sculpture, regularly accumulating piles of exhibition catalogues from all over the country.

A quiet and intense man with a very dry sense of humour, he still enjoys his painting very much and admits he could never give it up but believes that he has now achieved the correct balance between his painting and his private life.

In conclusion it must be said that the old adage of the artist being in love with his model remains an accurate observation and Michael is proof of that. To paint successfully an artist needs to form a relationship with his subject, irrespective of the subject being animal, vegetable or mineral. In Michael's case his muse which has unceasingly inspired him for over forty years has been one of the most popular of all models, and one we can all acknowledge, the beautiful English countryside.

Self-portrait – Motorcyclist

Publications

art of Alexander Gallery's role as Michael's agents was to market and distribute his paintings to galleries throughout the country and, as a consequence of this, over the last thirty years or so, Michael has built up a nationwide following of loyal collectors through this network of leading galleries. Another facet to this relationship has been in bringing his work to a wider audience through signed limited-edition reproductions of his paintings. A leading print publisher had already published a small number of his vividly coloured sky landscapes with some success before Alexander Gallery released 'The Four Seasons' in 1977.

These four small prints, 'Spring Comes To Winterbourne', 'Summer at Llandenny', 'Autumn' and 'The Beauty of Winter, Bolton Bridge' were all reproduced from small oil paintings. As a contrast to the large-scale panoramas Michael's smaller paintings have a more intimate feel of some house or farm stumbled upon by accident.

Since 'The Four Seasons' a further ten signed limited editions have followed, covering locations as far afield as Goathland in Yorkshire, Litlington in Sussex and Lerryn in Cornwall.

Pictures are not specifically painted for reproduction. Both publisher and artist feel this is too contrived, lacking artistic integrity and spontaneity. The decision to publish is more often than not based upon the immediate response to a picture by both the gallery and collectors alike. This is particularly true at an exhibition where often there will be just one picture that everyone seems to like and want to buy. 'Malpas Point' is a perfect example of this; it was the cover of Michael's 1993 exhibition at Alexander Gallery and everyone admired it. The painting sold immediately the exhibition opened and the subsequent limited edition sold out very quickly after publication. The signed limited edition prints by Michael Barnfather, illustrated in this section, are currently available.

The Bridge at Wareham
15 x 25in   Edition size 850 copies

Finishing Touches, Litlington
12 x 24in   Edition size 850 copies

Magic Pool
13 x 18in   Edition size 850 copies

Walking the Dog, St Anthony
15 x 20in   Edition size 850 copies

Morning Stroll, Christchurch, Dorset
14 x 14in   Edition size 650 copies

St Clement, near Truro
14 x 14in   Edition size 650 copies

Goathland Village, 'Heartbeat' Country
13 x 27in   Edition size 650 copies

St Winnow, Cornwall
13 x 27in   Edition size 650 copies

Autumn, Lerryn, Cornwall
13 x 25in   Edition size 650 copies

A Gallery-Owner Recalls

Michael Mosley of Granby Gallery in Bakewell has been exhibiting Michael's paintings for many years, holding a one-man show every two years since 1980.

'I had the pleasure of meeting Michael's parents some time before I met Michael. It was some twenty-six years ago when I had my first Russell Flint exhibition in the Smithy Restaurant in Bakewell. Anticipating that visitors would ask who else did I exhibit, I had prepared a small collection of paintings by various artists in my premises above our stationer's shop nearby. Included in this collection were three paintings by Michael and I was delighted when Mrs Barnfarther called in on her way to the Smithy and saw her son's pictures. After she had expressed her joy and pride at seeing Michael's paintings on display, I told her that I had recently seen a superb winter scene of his in a house in Derbyshire. The subject of the painting was Pilsley, near Chatsworth, and as this was my birthplace I inquired if the owners would be prepared to sell me the picture. They replied that they did not want to sell it at that time but if they ever did they would give me first refusal. After twenty-six years I am still waiting!

However, unbeknown to me, Mrs Barnfather had retold the story to her son and through the kind offices of Jim Fardon at Alexander Gallery, by now Michael's agent, a wonderful large painting of Pilsley arrived in the spring of exactly the same view as the snowscene I had coveted. I assumed that Michael had taken the references from his previous material but visiting the village a few days later I came across a man leaning on his gate, whose cottage featured in my painting. After chatting for a while he said to me, "You must be the fellow who the artist came up from Bristol to paint a picture for a few weeks back." I was thrilled, honoured and not the least astonished that Michael had been to such lengths on my behalf. After this Michael's parents, both delightful people, were regular visitors to our gallery for the rest of their lives – they are sadly missed.

At that time it was Pratts of Derby who were the main outlet for Michael's paintings in the county. However, when he retired Mr Pratt advised all his clients to visit Granby Gallery in Bakewell, who would in future be handling Michael's work, a course of action I very much appreciated. It was from this time that I really got to know Michael. Jim Fardon was looking for a gallery in Derbyshire that could successfully stage a bi-annual exhibition to complement the bi-annual exhibition in Bristol. This meant that Michael's numerous supporters in Derbyshire would have the opportunity to enjoy his work and in September 1980 we held our first exhibition.

We invited clients and collectors to a preview on the Thursday evening before we opened officially on the Friday. Our guests enjoyed the cheese and wine and more particularly the paintings that in the main were of Derbyshire subjects. A very high proportion of the paintings were sold during the evening and through the weekend and following week, setting us all on a very successful course which I am delighted to say continues to this day.

Occasionally, feeling that he had discovered all the best scenes in North Derbyshire, Michael would say to me "Mike, you are Derbyshire-born and bred, how about us going out together to search new territory?" On these occasions I would defer to my wife, Dorothy, who has always had a sense of the right direction – rather like a migrating bird that always knows which way to go. Such arduous countryside expeditions always required sustenance and we would always make sure that as lunchtime approached we would be in the vicinity of some local hostelry.

On one memorable occasion I recall us stopping off in a local pub to be greeted by a very good client of mine who at this stage must have had at least six of Michael's paintings in his collection at home. Part of that particular morning's work had included Michael sketching a bridge very close to the pub, a scene which just happened to be a great favourite of my client's. "The painting will need a couple of figures at the foot of the bridge," said Michael. "I'll include you and your wife shall I?" My client was ecstatic at the thought of featuring in a Michael Barnfather painting! But the downside, Michael explained, was that the picture was intended for my forthcoming exhibition and could not be sold before the preview evening. "No problem," said the happy client, "I attend all the previews and know the procedure."

An invitation was sent in the usual manner and his reply, accepting, likewise. He also phoned me to say he would be waiting at the gallery door ready for the opening. It is till a mystery to me today that he did not come either that evening or the next day. Not wishing to contact him for fearing to appear the aggressive salesman, on the Saturday I sold it to someone else. On the Monday he suddenly arrived. "Come for the picture," he announced, throwing the door open with an air of authority indicating his mission. At that moment he saw the painting displayed close to the door and noticed the red 'sold' spot on it. "You can't sell that," he exclaimed, "you can't sell that – that's me and my wife in that picture." I didn't know whether to summon an ambulance, anticipating an impending heart attack, or summon Michael to see if he could paint another – a course of action I knew neither of us would support. In the event the situation was resolved when Michael agreed to paint the bridge from the other side and feature them once more. They were delighted with the result and we all remained good friends but he never did explain why he hadn't come to the preview!'

Approach to Painting

I've got a sixth sense about a location. Even if I can't see a subject immediately, as I drive along I get a feeling that if I go to a different position then maybe there would be a good subject there.

As this quote reveals, painting has now become quite intuitive for Michael. After many years of traversing the countryside he is able to seek out a subject almost unconsciously. 'It is something about the way buildings are grouped together; an irregularity or a quirk in their layout will immediately catch my eye.'

Inevitably for a landscape painter much of the work takes place out of doors in all winds and weathers, and Michael is no exception. He spends considerable time travelling and has clocked up many thousands of miles in his cars over the years.

Having found a village or farm that gives him the correct feeling he sets off to explore the scene fully. He will often have to circumnavigate the whole area before he discovers the ideal view and this usually means seeking out footpaths and walkways around the back of a village and even, occasionally, a spot of surreptitious trespassing although he avoids this as much as possible.

If I see a subject from a distance and it looks fine I still like to have a walk through it; through the lie of the land and around the buildings so I know what is there, even if it doesn't appear in the finished painting. It is important to me to get to know the subject as well as possible.

Often this idea of going deep into a subject pays extra dividends as a subject for a smaller painting will suggest itself as Michael accumulates information for the larger picture. These smaller paintings have a more intimate feel, often of a scene stumbled upon by accident which is frequently exactly what happens. If a location really works then Michael will return to it again to paint it from different angles and also at different times of the year. 'By repeated visits I get to know my subject much better, rather in the manner of a portrait painter getting to know his sitter.'

Being an avid skier Michael has a particular fondness for snow and is very attuned to the dramatic qualities it can lend to a picture. Snowscenes also give him the opportunity to use a little more paint to create the effect of drifting snow and heavy falls on roofs and buildings.

Weather conditions are important when taking in a view. A bright day without strong sunshine is ideal; too much sun means too much shadow and from a distance interesting detail can be hidden in shadow. After absorbing the view Michael makes sketches and takes notes, carefully recording the mood and the conditions prevalent on the day in question. The scene is then photographed in some detail. As he tends to take in as much subject-hunting as he can over the period of a few days, it is important to record the exact physical layout of the location in this way. He could not possibly record every element of a scene without the use of a camera because it would just be too time consuming.

Back in the studio he selects a view from the photos, often joining several together to create a panorama. He takes the photos in an overlapping sequence in order to do this. Referring to his notes and sketchbooks and pinning the photographs in front of him on the easel he will begin, having already decided what size canvas he wants to use. His most common canvas now is 15 or 16 inches high by 30 inches wide, a size and proportion that suits his work perfectly. The basic composition is sketched out in pencil before broad oil washes are applied.

As Michael paints recognisable and clearly stated locations, any manipulation of the scene is kept to an absolute minimum. He prefers to disguise with trees rather than omit unsightly aspects of the location, although telegraph poles are definitely removed. The careful placement of a tree or group of trees can also break up an area of too much stone or brickwork. Plain open foregrounds are distracting to the viewer and in these instances can be broken up by standing water or a pond, which can also introduce reflected light to add interest to the picture. Another device familiar to collectors of Michael's paintings is the broken branch. Originally introduced along with a cartwheel and a small flock of birds to give interest to an essentially static scene, the branch is often a pointer towards the prime part of the painting. These three trademarks have now become as much an element of Michael's paintings as his own signature and are looked for in very much in the way that Terence Cuneo's famous mouse was in all of his pictures.

Sketch – Cromford Pond, Derbyshire

Michael regards these devices not as 'artistic licence' but as subtle finishing touches to the scene he wishes to preserve. Another of these finishing touches is his use of figures. These are used to add an element of interest or mystery and to give a sense of movement to a painting. Often they are memories or a reminder of people who may have been present at some stage of Michael's deliberations. Although an integral part of the original composition, they are usually amongst the last elements of the painting to be completed.

In addition to his landscapes Michael also paints abstracts in oils, as well as the occasional watercolour, and he took the opportunity to paint a small group of watercolours for this book. The complete turn-around in technique in working with watercolours is 'nice for a change', enabling him to work quickly and on a fairly broad scale. Even so he still includes most of his trademarks and of course the subject matter is still recognisably 'Barnfather Country'.

As an insight to the way he works Michael talks us through the background to one of the paintings illustrated in this book.

The village of Milldale on the River Dove is one of my favourite Derbyshire locations. It is a village I know very well through repeat visits over many years and has provided me with lots of enjoyment over the years. Every time I visit Derbyshire on a painting trip I make a point of visiting Milldale in the hope I might just happen upon a new aspect of the village. Of course the scene alters anyway over the years as the trees mature and vary according the seasons. As far as I know I have been all around the village and must have painted at least seven pictures from different angles and at different times of the year, especially the autumn.

On this occasion I liked the lead in to the village across the bridge, following the path that comes in from the left-hand side of the painting. As a subject it is a bit more complicated than some of the other views of the village I've painted and I must confess, although it is a scene that had always appealed to me, I had put off painting it before. However, I thought it would be an ideal subject for this book and I took the opportunity to take a series of photographs showing the stage by stage progression.

1. The essential aspects of the composition are roughly sketched in with pencil on a primed blank canvas.

2. Washes of colour are added to kill the whiteness of the canvas, leaving the outline of the buildings and the horizon clearly visible.

3. Most of the canvas is now covered in broad blocks of paint. The tree area is filled in with dark greens which will allow Michael to work from dark to light. It is at this point that Michael really begins to get the feel of the picture.

4. The scene begins to take shape as more detailing and form is added to the bridge and the buildings. Reflections appear in the water and a little more is made of the foreground.

5. After a lot more work in the trees and the sky the direction and effect of the sunlight is much more apparent. The foreground is left untouched as no final decision has been made on the positioning of the figures.

6. Figures begin to appear, in the village and on the bridge, and there is a suggestion of a walking figure on the foreground path.

7. The finished painting, now including the walker on the path who has actually been moved from his initial position closer to the bridge in the original pencil sketch.

The Paintings

Of all the parts of the British Isles that Michael has painted, it is the county of Derbyshire that remains his first love, as the following collection of paintings testify.

Author's Note: *The more observant may notice that one or two of the subjects that follow may not lie within the strict county confines of Derbyshire; in these circumstances it has always been my experience that Michael regards the elasticity of such boundaries as being one of the rights in holding a valid artistic licence.*

Michael usually manages to set aside time each year for one very large painting, either
an 18 x 48in canvas or, as in this instance, a 24 x 48in canvas. Such pictures are by their
nature very complex compositions and can take him up to a month to paint.
This particular picture is available as an unlimited fine art print.

Testing the Ice, Monyash Village
Oil 24 x 48in

Autumn Colour, Ladybooth, near Castleton
Oil 15 x 42in

Yew Tree Grange, near Sterndale, Derbyshire
Oil 18 x 36in

Country Matters, Alport
Oil 12 x 18in

A dramatic winter scene in which the foreground is especially effective with a real feeling of depth to the snow created by liberal application of paint. Unusually for Michael the village is hidden away somewhat as if it has just been stumbled upon by accident.

Winter's Mantle, Beeley
Oil 16 x 22in

Spring Comes to Elton Village
Oil 18 x 48in

Bradbourne Mill
Oil 16 x 22in

Fetch it Rover, the Wye in Spate
Oil 18 x 14in

A Derbyshire Farm, near Melbourne
Oil 15 x 42

View over Beeley
Oil 18 x 36in

The five paintings of the village of Tissington in this book illustrate perfectly

Michael's ability to explore fully and then absorb a location before painting it

from a variety of views and during different times of the year.

A Corner of Tissington
Oil 16 x 22in

The Short Cut, Tissington
Oil 15 x 42in

View, near Winster
Oil 15 x 30in

'As usual I walked all around the scene before settling on this view which I thought
was the most interesting with the quarry behind the houses.'

Peveril Castle, Castleton
Oil 16 x 16in

'Although I have painted numerous pictures of Derbyshire I am always surprised and delighted to find new subjects. However this painting is in fact a later version of a subject I first painted many years ago. It is a very simple composition and sometimes I feel these often turn out well; and I remember how many people liked the finished painting.'

Bridge at Milldale
Oil 12 x 18in

One of Michael's favourite Derbyshire villages, on this occasion under a full covering of snow.

The composition here is very satisfying on the eye as the viewer is led straight

into the village by the curve of the foreground wall.

I Will Tell You a Secret, Tissington
Oil 20 x 30in

Another example of how one location can provide widely differing perspectives.

Compare this almost ground-level view of the bridge at Milldale with

Summer Pleasures, Viator's Bridge on page 111

Viator's Bridge, Milldale
Oil 16 x16in

Exploring Tissington
Oil 15 x 42in

Alstonefield Church, Looking East
Oil 15 x 42in

'There had been a couple of local break-ins shortly before I arrived in the village looking for painting references and I suddenly found myself confronted by a rather belligerent farmer convinced that this rather suspicious looking man with a camera was up to no good! After I had explained what I was doing and why, his manner totally altered and he became very pleasant towards me with the upshot that he requested an invitation to my next exhibition in Bakewell – but whether he attended or not I don't know'.

Snow at Monyash
Oil 18 x 24

Cottage at Black Rocks, Overlooking Cromford
Oil 12 x 18in

The Meadows, Bakewell
Oil 14 x 18in

This square format is a relatively new departure for Michael and gives him the chance to record the intimacy of an encounter or event that would otherwise be lost within one of his larger panoramas.

Autumn Chat, Middleton
Oil 16 x 16in

'I wanted to try something a bit different with this picture and get away from green

fields and pale skies and create the perspective of the fields by contrasting the strong

gold colour against the intensity of the darker sky.'

Autumn Colour, Carlton Lees
Oil 14 x 14in

A rare case of Michael using a fair amount of artistic licence in order to reveal the delightful church, most of which is actually hidden away behind houses.

Is This the Way? Hathersage Church
Oil 14 x 18in

'I remember this scene from my childhood and it hasn't changed very much in all those years. Although I have painted it before this is the first time from this particular viewpoint'.

The Pond at Cromford
Oil 14 x 18in

Through the Trees, Tissington
Oil 18 x 36in

BARNFATHER

Picnic at Swarkestone
Oil 15 x 30in

BARNFATHER

The Ambush, near Doveholes
Oil 16 x 30in

The Bandstand, Buxton
Oil 14 x 14in

Winter Fun, Alstonefield
Oil 12 x 20in

BARNFATHER

Lead Mill Bridge, Hathersage
Oil 15 x 30in

'Whilst I was taking references for this painting my ears were bombarded with very loud pop music coming from a rehearsal in a nearby barn, which totally disturbed my concentration at the time. Despite this intrusion into my quiet deliberations the area itself provided me with enough good material for a couple of pictures.'

View near Ashover
Oil 15 x 30in

BARNFATHER

Across the Meadows at Bakewell
Oil 15 x 30in

The Conversation, Ashford in the Water
Oil 16 x 30in

The Ride Home, Tissington
Oil 15 x 30in

Another view of Alstonefield but at a very different time of year. All the usual Barnfather trademarks are in evidence in this delightful little painting, including the 'puddle' that gently breaks the foreground, yet in no way do any of them detract from a very satisfying composition.

A Quiet Chat, Autumn, Alstonefield
Oil 12 x 20in

'A popular spot, especially with children in the summer.

Even when the river dries up in parts there nearly always

seems to be water here held in place rather like a dam.'

Crossing the Swimming Hole, Bradford Dale
Oil 14 x 18in

'We had a nice run up by the reservoir one day in early spring and as we were driving along I caught some interesting glimpses through the trees. Stopping the car we walked through the woods to find an open view and as soon as we found one I was immediately struck by the tranquillity of the water and the peacefulness of the entire scene.'

Touch of Snow, Derwent Reservoir
Oil 20 x 30in

Tea Time, Ashford in the Water
Oil 16 x 30in

BARNFATHER

The White Stuff, Bradford Dale
Oil 20 x 40in

The little twin arched bridge that spans the River Dove at Milldale takes its name from the character in Izaak Walton's classic text on the art of angling, *The Compleat Angler* who said, 'why a mouse can hardly go over it, it is only two fingers broad'.

Summer Pleasures, Viator's Bridge
Oil 18 x 24in

The following seven watercolours were all painted especially for this book. The complete about-face in painting technique means that Michael has to paint quickly working 'wet on wet' and on a fairly broad basis. Like his abstracts these watercolours provide him with a break from working in great detail with oils.

Private, Ashford Hall Fishing
Watercolour 10 x 14in

View from the New Bridge, Bakewell
Watercolour 11 x 15in

Peak Distric View
Watercolour 11 x 15in

Viator's Bridge, Milldale
Watercolour 11 x 15in

River Bradford at Alport
Watercolour 14 x 18in

Derwent Reservoir, Looking Towards Howden Reservoir
Watercolour 14 x 18in

A Corner of Derwent Reservoir
Watercolour 10 x 14in

The Packhorse Bridge, Ashford in the Water
Oil 10 x 18in

Ashbourne Church
Oil 20 x 30in

View over Winster
Oil 18 x 48in

Edmaston from Brailsford, near Ashbourne
Oil 15 x 42in

Mayfield Church, near Ashover
Oil 15 x 42in

Blore Church and Farm
Oil 15 x 30in

This picture is one of a small group of paintings commissioned by a Derbyshire collector. Michael is not averse to taking on such commissions provided he feels he is able to do justice to the subject and the requirements of the client. In this instance the task was interesting for him because of the diverse range of subjects required by the client.

Tom Moore's Cottage
Oil 15 x 30in

Saw Mills, Osmaston
Oil 16 x 22in

Mill Dale
Oil 12 x 18in

Sheepwash Bridge, Ashford in the Water
Oil 18 x 36in

The use of sunlight and strong shadow create depth and structure in this painting.
It is very much a walker's picture, recording the moment the village is reached
after a long afternoon of fresh air and wonderful views.

The Stile, Tissington
Oil 16 x 16in

A story picture. Through the title the figures, although small, become

the immediate point of focus before the viewer 'steps back' to take in the

panaroma and the considerable detail of the buildings.

Hope it Doesn't Bite, Beeley
Oil 16 x 30in

Michael has used a mixture of horizontal and vertical shapes to make this picture rather interesting and there is plenty for the eye to seek out in the composition.

The Road from Bakewell to Monyash
Oil 16 x 16in

'Painted snow is never pure white. Like the real thing it is a mixture of colours and tones and often has an almost abstract feel to it, rather like the foreground in this picture.'

Winter at Winster
Oil 10 x 20in

Spring at Dovedale
Oil 14 x 18in

144